KEY TO COUNTERING ISLAMIC FUNDAMENTALISM

NCRI PRESIDENT-ELECT MARYAM RAJAVI

TESTIMONY TO THE U.S. HOUSE FOREIGN AFFAIRS COMMITTEE, SUBCOMMITTEE ON TERRORISM, NONPROLIFERATION AND TRADE

APRIL 29, 2015

MARYAM RAJAVI TESTIMONY BEFORE THE U.S. CONGRESS;
Regime Change in Iran by the Iranian People Key to Countering Islamic Fundamentalism

First published in 2015 by
National Council of Resistance of Iran - U.S. Representative Office
1747 Pennsylvania Ave., NW, Suite 1125, Washington, DC 20006

ISBN-13: 978-0-9904327-2-2
ISBN-10: 0-9904327-2-2

Library of Congress Cataloging-in-Publication Data
National Council of Resistance of Iran - U.S. Representative Office.

MARYAM RAJAVI TESTIMONY BEFORE THE U.S. CONGRESS;
Regime Change in Iran by the Iranian People Key to Countering Islamic Fundamentalism

1. Iran-Islamic fundamentalism. 2. Nuclear weapons-Iran.
3. Iran-Foreign relations. 4. Security, International. 5. ISIS.

First Edition: May 2015
Printed in the United States of America

TABLE OF CONTENTS

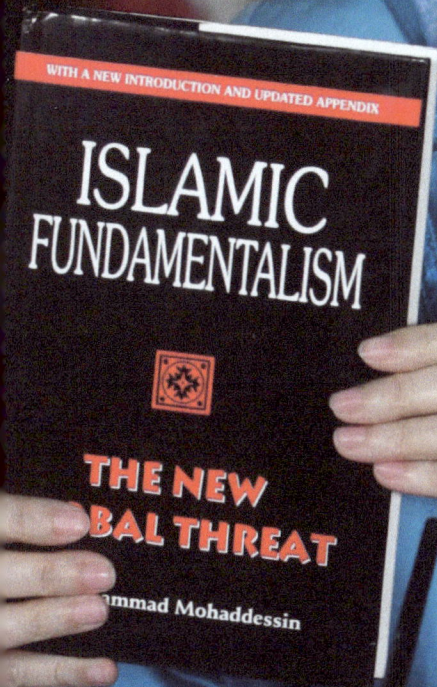

WITH A NEW INTRODUCTION AND UPDATED APPENDIX

ISLAMIC
FUNDAMENTALISM

THE NEW
BAL THREAT

mmad Mohaddessin

NCRI President-elect Maryam Rajavi to U.S. House Hearing: Regime Change in Iran by the Iranian People Key to Countering Islamic Fundamentalism

On April 29, 2015, Mrs. Maryam Rajavi, the president of the National Council of Resistance of Iran, appeared via videoconference in a hearing titled "ISIS: Defining the Enemy" held by the House Foreign Affairs Subcommittee on Terrorism, Nonproliferation and Trade.

In her remarks, Mrs. Rajavi offered an in-depth analysis of Islamic Fundamentalism and recommended an alternative approach to counter it, which would include overturning the theocratic regime in Tehran. Maryam Rajavi outlined several practical steps that Western governments might take toward this end, one of which was to "recognize the Iranian people's aspirations to overthrow the mullahs." She emphasized that the mullahs' regime is not part of any solution to current crises; it is indeed the heart of the problem.

She told the U.S. Congress that in the "absence of a firm policy vis-à-vis the regime in Tehran, there will be destructive consequences."

Mrs. Rajavi referred to the Iranian regime as the "epicenter of fundamentalism" in the Middle East adding that "Islamic fundamentalism emerged as a threat to peace and security when Khomeini stole the leadership of a popular revolution in 1979 and established a religious dictatorship."

The Iranian opposition leader also said: "The Iranian regime has served as the main source of this ominous phenomenon in the region and across the world. The primary objective of Islamic fundamentalists, including ISIS, is to establish an Islamic Caliphate and enforce Sharia law."

"Owing to the pivotal role of the People's Mojahedin Organization of Iran (PMOI/MEK) as a democratic Muslim movement, the Iranian Resistance has established itself as the antithesis to Islamic fundamentalism." "To counter Islamic fundamentalists, democratic and tolerant Islam should be empowered," she explained.

PAGE 2

NCRI President Remarks in the Congressional Hearing on Islamic Fundamentalism
National Council of Resistance of Iran • U.S. Representative Office (NCRI-US)

MRS. RAJAVI OUTLINED THE FOLLOWING PRACTICAL STEPS NECESSARY FOR DEFEATING ISLAMIC FUNDAMENTALISM

1   **Expel** the Quds Force from Iraq and end the Iranian regime's influence in that country.

2   **Enable** full participation of Sunnis in power sharing and arm Sunni tribes to provide security for their communities.

3   **Assist** Syria's moderate opposition and people to end Assad's regime and establish democracy in that country.

4   **Recognize** the Iranian people's aspirations to overthrow the mullahs and end inaction vis-à-vis the gross human rights violations in Iran.

5   **Provide** protection for, and uphold the rights of members of Iran's organized opposition, the MEK, residing in Camp Liberty in Iraq.

6   **Empower** the true, democratic and tolerant Islam to counter fundamentalist interpretations of this religion.

7   **Block** all pathways for the Iranian regime to acquire nuclear weapons.

TESTIMONY OF
MRS. MARYAM RAJAVI
PRESIDENT-ELECT OF THE
NATIONAL COUNCIL
OF RESISTANCE OF IRAN

Text of Testimony by Mrs. Maryam Rajavi,
The President-elect of the National Council of Resistance of Iran

Submitted to:
The House Foreign Affairs Committee,
Subcommittee on Terrorism, Nonproliferation and Trade

April 29, 2015

Mr. Chairman, Ranking Member,
Distinguished members of the Committee,

Thank you for giving me this opportunity to speak to you.

Today, Islamic fundamentalism and extremism, in the name of ISIS or Shiite paramilitary groups, have launched a vicious onslaught against territories spanning from East Asia to the southern and eastern shores of the Mediterranean, sparing neither the Americas nor Europe.

For 36 years, we have resisted a religious tyranny, driven by Islamic fundamentalism, and fought for democracy in Iran.

Before getting into the details, allow me to briefly touch upon a few points:

1   Islamic fundamentalism and extremism emerged as a threat to regional and global peace and tranquility after a religious dictatorship (based on the principle of the *velayat-e faqih*, or absolute rule of the clergy) came to power in Iran in 1979. Since then, the regime in Tehran has acted as the driving force for, and the epicenter of, this ominous phenomenon regionally and worldwide.

2   The primary objective of fundamentalism is to establish an Islamic Empire (or Caliphate) and enforce Sharia law by force. It neither recognizes any boundaries nor differentiates between Sunnis and Shiites. Aggressiveness and the penchant for violence primarily characterize Islamic fundamentalism. As such, searching for moderates among its adherents is an illusion.

3 In 1993, we published a book entitled, "Islamic Fundamentalism; the New Global Threat,"[1] warning about this menace and identifying its epicenter as Tehran. We reiterated that the clerical regime sought to acquire the nuclear bomb in order to export its reactionary ideology and to guarantee its own survival. Regrettably, this threat was not taken seriously. The experience of the past three decades shows that in the absence of a firm policy vis-à-vis the regime in Tehran, the world will face destructive consequences.

4 Unfortunately, the failure to thwart the Iranian regime's post-2003 meddling in Iraq enabled it to gradually occupy that country, propelling the unprecedented spread of extremism. Similarly, the atrocities perpetrated by (the Islamic Revolutionary Guards Corps') Quds Force in Syria and Iraq (to prop up Tehran's puppets, Bashar al-Assad and Nuri al-Maliki), and the massacre and the exclusion of Sunnis, coupled with Western silence, empowered ISIS.

5 I reiterate that the mullahs' regime is not part of any solution as we attempt to deal with Islamic fundamentalism; it is indeed the heart of the problem.

The ultimate solution to this problem is regime change by the Iranian people and Resistance.

This regime is extremely fragile and vulnerable. As evident during the 2009 uprising, the overwhelming majority of the Iranian people yearn for fundamental change, i.e. ending the theocratic regime and the establishment of democracy.

The regime's show of force is hollow and a consequence of feeble Western policy. It is intended to mask the mullahs' underlying inability to meet the demands of millions of Iranians in the 21st century.

Owing to the pivotal role of the People's Mojahedin Organization of Iran (PMOI/MEK) as a democratic Muslim movement, the Iranian Resistance has established itself as the antithesis to Islamic fundamentalism.

PAGE 8

NCRI President Remarks in the Congressional Hearing on Islamic Fundamentalism
National Council of Resistance of Iran • U.S. Representative Office (NCRI-US)

We can and we must defeat Islamic fundamentalism, whether the Shiite or the Sunni variants of it. Forming an international coalition and taking the following practical steps are indispensable to achieve this goal:

1. **Expel the Quds Force from Iraq** thus ending the Iranian regime's influence in that country. Enable genuine participation of the Sunnis in power sharing and arm Sunni tribes to empower them to provide security for their communities;

2. **Assist Syria's moderate opposition and people** to end Assad's tyrannical rule and establish democracy in that country;

3. **Recognize the Iranian people's aspirations** to overthrow the mullahs' regime and end inaction vis-à-vis the flagrant abuses of human rights in Iran. Provide protection for, and uphold the rights of, the residents of Camp Liberty (members of the PMOI/MEK) in Iraq;

4. **Empower the genuine, democratic, and tolerant Islam** to counter fundamentalist interpretations of this religion; and

5. **Block all pathways** for the Iranian regime to acquire nuclear weapons.

Mr. Chairman,

The discourse about Islamic extremism, which has emerged as a long-standing global threat, and which has launched a wide-ranging assault on the achievements of human civilization, is not merely an academic or a theoretical exercise. Rather, the aim, here, is to find a viable and practical solution to safeguard humanity from this sinister phenomenon.

With the rise of ISIS and escalation of the crises in Iraq, Syria and Yemen, Islamic extremism has grown more vexing in recent months. But, for the Iranian people and Resistance this was not an unknown peril. Following the collapse of the Soviet Union and the 1991 Persian Gulf War, the Resistance warned that Islamic fundamentalism had emerged as the new global threat. Regrettably, this menace was not taken seriously.

Today, bloodied corpses of young school girls in Pakistan, kidnapping of innocent women and girls in Nigeria, beheading defenseless youth and forcible displacement of thousands of people in Iraq and Syria, appalling massacre of Sunnis in Iraq and their kidnapping, displacement, and forcible resettlement, terrorist attacks in Paris and Copenhagen, atrocious persistence and escalation of executions in Iran, coupled with the slaughter and imprisonment of religious minorities, have all deeply horrified the conscience of contemporary humanity.

Now, the people in the Middle East, Europe and elsewhere in the world are confronted with the greatest threat to the contemporary era: the challenge of extremism masquerading as Islam.

The question is: what is the main cause for the creation and rise of Islamic fundamentalism and where is its epicenter? Is the Shiite variant of extremism different from the Sunni one? Was the spread of such a malignant cancer inevitable? And finally, could this ominous phenomenon be defeated, and, if yes, what is the strategy to defeat it?

It is critical to answer these questions because they can serve as a guide to identify the solution and adopt the appropriate policies in dealing with this ominous phenomenon.

THE MAIN CAUSE FOR THE EMERGENCE AND EXPANSION OF FUNDAMENTALISM

The *velayat-e faqih* system that the founder of the Iranian regime, Khomeini, established after usurping the leadership of a popular revolution in Iran - made possible because the Shah's regime had suppressed the democratic and progressive movements and imprisoned their leadership - created for the first time in contemporary history a state that combined political power with "religious" authority: a medieval tyranny hiding behind the curtain of religion.

The ultimate and declared goal of fundamentalists has been to establish an Islamic Caliphate and enforce Sharia law by force. This objective is the common denominator and the focal point of all variants of Islamic fundamentalism whether Sunni or Shiite, which render their differences secondary in light of such commonality of purpose. Khomeini dubbed this as *"velayat-e motlaq-e faqih"* (absolute rule of the clergy), emphasizing that preserving "Islamic" rule took precedence over everything else.

This phenomenon is distinctly characterized by its aggressiveness and propensity for violence. It does not recognize any boundaries and its survival hinges on expansion. For this reason, from day one, the regime resorted to killings, torture and daily executions, coupled with stoning, eye-gouging and limb amputation, which have continued to this date. Simultaneously, it embarked on meddling in the affairs of other countries.

The *velayat-e faqih* system is incongruent with today's world, the people's needs and contemporary developments, and is incapable of resolving any political, social, economic or cultural problems in the 21st century. It therefore relies solely on naked violence, under the veneer of Islam, to prolong itself. The mullahs are intent on turning back the clock through sheer force, violence, and slaughter, which explains why they perpetrate countless atrocities.

Inside Iran, the mullahs eliminated women from political and social participation. Through discrimination, brutal crackdown, and imposition of mandatory veiling, they tried to intimidate and terrorize the citizenry. Under the banner of "cultural revolution" they shut down all universities for three years in order to set up educational entities totally in line with their own whims. They closed all newspapers that were critical of their policies and banned all dissident organizations, parties, and political entities.

Ethnic minorities were subjected to severe suppression and discrimination and religious minorities were brutally oppressed and deprived of their basic rights. This criminal conduct was quickly enshrined in the Constitution and institutionalized in the penal and civil codes, and continues today.

This is precisely the example, which both Sunni and Shiite extremists are following in other countries. This system of governance completely contradicts Islam and civilized norms. It is called an "Islamic Caliphate" by Sunni fundamentalists who adhere to the very same attributes and modus operandi. From a legal and religious standpoint, this system lacks the slightest capacity to change from within. The regime eliminates anyone challenging the absolute rule of the clergy.

As stipulated in its Constitution, the clerical regime formed the Revolutionary Guard Corps to protect the *velayat-e faqih* system and to expand it to other parts of the Islamic world.[2] It also created 75 different repressive agencies to leash and to suppress the public. To date, it has executed 120,000 political dissidents, ranging from 13-year-old girls to pregnant women and the elderly.[3]

Export of this medieval mindset, or, as Khomeini called it, export of revolution, is indispensable and inherent to the regime's modus operandi. The Iranian Resistance's leader Massoud Rajavi explained the principal theory behind the

NCRI President Remarks in the Congressional Hearing on Islamic Fundamentalism
National Council of Resistance of Iran • U.S. Representative Office (NCRI-US)

policy of exporting fundamentalism on several occasions. Incapable of guiding the enormous energy unleashed in the anti-monarchic revolution towards freedom, democracy and development, Khomeini squandered part of it in the war with Iraq and directed the rest outside the country under the pretext of 'exporting revolution,' he said.

> In reality, the existence of a tremendously young and restless society that overthrew the previous dictatorship has rendered this medieval regime permanently unstable, compelling it to export its backward ideology in order to put a lid on its internal crises.

In the Iranian regime's Constitution, the export of crisis, terrorism and fundamentalism has been codified in Articles 3, 11, and 154 under the guise of "relentless support for the *Mustazafan* (world's oppressed)" and "unity in the Islamic world." These are among the pillars of the regime's foreign policy.[4]

For Khomeini, exporting "Islamic revolution" to, and establishing a sister regime in Iraq was the first order of business. Doing so set the stage for a conflict that subsequently erupted when Iraq attacked Iran in 1980. By trying to dominate Iraq as early as in 1979 and subsequently perpetuating the unpatriotic Iran-Iraq war—with the mantra of "liberating Quds (Jerusalem) via Karbala—the regime sought to export its medieval ideology to the Islamic world. In contrast, the international community and the United Nations Security Council demanded an end to the war and called for a ceasefire. Khomeini had correctly realized that Iraq could be used as the springboard for encroaching upon the Arab and the Islamic world.

The enclosed map, published by the Revolutionary Guards Corps in the mid-1980s, exposes Khomeini's designs, in the midst of the Iran-Iraq War, to turn Iraq into a beachhead to dominate the Islamic world. Khomeini lost that war. But the international community's failure to grasp and understand the regime's nature and intentions and the resultant misguided policies in dealing with it, enabled Khomeini's successors to achieve that goal. Looking now, you can see that the regime has tried to encroach upon the very countries that it coveted to dominate in the early 1980s.

Khomeini had to accept defeat in the Iran-Iraq war in 1988. To prevent any social backlash he ordered the massacre of over 30,000 political prisoners in a matter of a few months. A majority of the victims belonged to PMOI/MEK, which ironically were Shiite Muslims.[5]

Today, the very officials responsible for the 1988 massacre occupy key positions in government agencies, including in Hassan Rouhani's cabinet and the regime's Judiciary.[6]

Parallel with the war with Iraq and particularly afterwards, the Iranian regime allocated an enormous budget to set up the so-called cultural and educational centers in different countries for the purpose of propagating its extremist ideology and recruiting adherents. In many places, including Lebanon, Palestinian territories, Syria, Iraq, and Yemen, it trained, funded, and armed both Shiite and Sunni terrorists.

From the outset, the clerical regime tried to spread extremism by taking 52 Americans hostage for 444 days in 1979, blowing up the U.S. Marines barracks in Beirut in 1983, creating Hezbollah in Lebanon and the Supreme Council for Islamic Revolution in Iraq (SCIRI group) as well as a number of groups in other Muslim majority countries, and taking western citizens hostage in Lebanon.

This policy is not restricted to the past. In recent years, the policy of meddling in other countries' affairs has indeed intensified, taking on significantly deeper and broader dimensions. As such, fundamentalism acquired both a new form and broader dimensions, and grew by leveraging the unique cultural and historical standing of Iran, a country that has also been endowed with one of the world's largest oil and gas reserves.

In reality, Iran became the cultural capital of the Islamic world in the early decades after the advent of Islam so much so that any transformation or change in Iran has had an auxiliary impact on the world of Islam during the past 14 centuries. After Khomeini came to power, however, he placed Iran on a different path and transformed it into the epicenter of fundamentalism, crowning it as the godfather of extremists and terrorists in the Middle East.

PAGE 14

NCRI President Remarks in the Congressional Hearing on Islamic Fundamentalism
National Council of Resistance of Iran • U.S. Representative Office (NCRI-US)

It was only through the existence of the *velayat-e faqih* regime in Iran that Islamic fundamentalism morphed into a new global threat. Without the instrument of state power in a country like Iran, reactionary forces would not have mustered such potential and prospect to emerge as a destructive force.

This transformation would have been impossible without the central role of Iran, a vast, rich country situated in a strategic location and known for its unique influence in the Islamic world. Conversely, the collapse of this epicenter leads to the isolation and defeat of this ominous threat across the globe and renders it ineffectual.

FLAWED DICHOTOMY BETWEEN SHIITE AND SUNNI FUNDAMENTALISM

Contrary to the realities underscored above, because ISIS and Sunni fundamentalist groups do not have a perceivable and clear link to the mullahs in Tehran and are hostile to one another in a number of areas, an artificial dichotomy has been assumed between Sunni and Shiite fundamentalists. Some policymakers and pundits therefore even view the Iranian regime as a potential partner in the fight against ISIS.

Meanwhile, Tehran's clerical rulers are expediently using both Sunni and Shiite extremist groups for the regime's own purposes. They direct Lebanon's Hezbollah and arm extremist Sunni groups in Arab countries. Over the past 20 years and at many important junctures, the Iranian regime provided enormous assistance to Sunni extremists like Al Qaeda.

Since 2001, Tehran has provided safe haven to a number of Al Qaeda leaders, later facilitating their passage to Iraq, Syria, and other Muslim countries.

In February 2012, the regime's Supreme Leader Ali Khamenei emphasized, "The Islamic Revolution has a mandatory religious obligation to equally help both the Sunni and Shiite jihadists."[7]

On June 4, 2014, only three days before ISIS took over Mosul, Khamenei made a public speech in which he said: "Don't make a mistake. The enemy is America. *Takfiri* groups are just seditionists."[8] In the Iranian regime's lexicon, the loyal opposition is described as seditionist.

More importantly, if it were not for the Iranian regime's domination of Iraq, the sectarian policies of its puppet prime minister Nuri al-Maliki, and the massacre committed against the Sunni population in Iraq, and if it were not for the slaughter of 250,000 people in Syria by the Assad regime and the Iranian regime's Quds Force, ISIS would have never been able to find such a fertile breeding ground for its emergence and expansion.

In his will, Khomeini called for the overthrow of all existing governments in the Muslim world, followed by the eviction of their rulers, and establishment of "one Islamic State with free and independent republics."[9] The regime's current leader Khamenei declared himself the source of emulation for Shiites and the Supreme Leader for all Muslims. In other words, as it pertains to governance, Khamenei considers himself the ruler of all Muslims.[10]

The terrorist Quds Force, formed a quarter of a century ago, is the instrument for exporting extremism to not only Shiite but also to Sunni communities.

Theoretically speaking, fundamentalism represents a perverted view of Islam. What is presented under the banner of these two aberrations in the Islamic faith, are in essence one and the same thing. Both emphasize misogyny and religious discrimination. Both, impose religion and beliefs through the use of force, contrary to Quranic verses; both rely on the laws of past millennia called Sharia to enforce the most violent and inhumane forms of punishment; both pursue a reactionary caliphate, which translates into the cruel rule of an individual tyrant. One calls it the *velayat-e motlaq-e faqih* (the absolute rule of clergy) while the other refers to it as a Caliph. Of course, three decades ago,

PAGE 16

NCRI President Remarks in the Congressional Hearing on Islamic Fundamentalism
National Council of Resistance of Iran • U.S. Representative Office (NCRI-US)

Khomeini explicitly said in a public speech that "We want a Caliph who would amputate limbs, flog and stone to death."[11]

Shiite fundamentalists, however, are more dangerous than their Sunni counterparts because they rely on a regional power, namely the religious dictatorship ruling Iran. Look at the situation in Iraq and what is happening there on a daily basis. The mullahs' so-called Shiite militias act more viciously than their Sunni equivalents, such as ISIS. In the long run, they pose a much greater threat than their Sunni brethren to Iraq's independent existence and regional peace, security, and stability. With the help of these militias, the mullahs have turned four Arab countries into theaters of their terrorism and destruction.

The militia groups in Iraq, the Hezbollah in Lebanon, and the Houthis in Yemen are under total control and backing of the mullahs' Revolutionary Guards Corps (IRGC) and Khamenei. The Iranian regime is Bashar Assad's main patron and the primary factor for keeping him in power is Syria. In September 2014, a member of mullahs' parliament (Majlis) said, "Currently, three Arab capitals are in the hands of Iran, and Sana'a will be the fourth... We seek the unification of Islamic countries."[12]

A Friday prayer leader added that the borders of the Islamic Republic had reached Yemen.[13] A number of the highest ranking regime officials, including Khamenei's senior advisor, explicitly and publicly called Syria an Iranian province.[14]

In short, the regime ruling Iran is the axis of Islamic fundamentalism in terms of ideology, policies, money, weapons, and logistical support. Beyond any form of concrete political or financial link between these sorts of groups and Tehran, the determining factor is the presence of a fundamentalist regime in power in Iran (the *velayat-e faqih*), which presents a model and inspires the formation of all fundamentalist groups and cells. In the absence of such a regime, there would be no intellectual, ideological, or political space, or a central base and dependable epicenter for the emergence and growth of such groups.

As long as the Tehran regime is not replaced by a democratic, tolerant, and pluralist government, the problem of Islamic fundamentalism will persist regardless of any military and security confrontation, every time emerging in different variations.

THE NUCLEAR BOMB IN THE POLICY OF EXPORT OF FUNDAMENTALISM AND TERRORISM

Nuclear weapons serve both to guarantee the survival of the Iranian regime and pave the way for exporting fundamentalism.

The clerical regime's former president and current head of the Expediency Council Ali-Akbar Hashemi Rafsanjani, boasted in the early 1990s, "If we acquire nuclear weapons, who could prevent the export of the revolution to Islamic countries?"

Khamenei's fatwa about nuclear weapons being haram (forbidden) is a hoax. Many years ago, Khomeini reminded Khamenei that the *vali-e faqih* (supreme ruler) has the power to unilaterally abrogate his religious commitments to the citizenry if that were to serve the interests of the state.

> By acquiring a nuclear bomb, the Iranian regime seeks to upend the regional balance of power and subsequently exert its hegemony over the whole region. To be sure, a nuclear-armed or nuclear threshold regime in Iran will propel an arms race across the region; but this is only the lesser consequence. The primary fallout would be the Iranian regime's domination of the political, economic, and military disposition of the region and of many Muslim countries.

It would be a fatal mistake to believe that silence and accommodation vis-à-vis the regime's onslaught throughout the region would help advance the nuclear talks. Tehran is intimating this approach in different ways and, of course, has so far taken full advantage of it to advance its designs both regarding its nuclear projects and meddling in the region. Firmness in dealing with the regime will force it to retreat. Giving concessions to it, on the other hand, will embolden it to be more aggressive.

NCRI President Remarks in the Congressional Hearing on Islamic Fundamentalism

National Council of Resistance of Iran • U.S. Representative Office (NCRI-US)

NUCLEAR PROGRAM: NATIONAL PRIDE OR SPREADING FUNDAMENTALISM IN THE REGION?

To describe the mullahs' nuclear weapons program as a source of "national pride" is an affront to the Iranian people who believe otherwise. Using this pretext to offer concessions to the clerics is therefore unacceptable. The mullahs seek to obtain nuclear weapons to preserve their regime and export their reactionary mindset to the region, both of which are contrary to the interests and yearnings of the Iranian people.

> Iran does not need nuclear energy because it does not make economic sense! The clerical regime has invested hundreds of billions of dollars in this program while lack of sufficient investment in the oil industry has left the country without adequate refineries, compelling it to import gasoline from abroad. This is tantamount to a disaster. [15]

Our 36-year experience has made it palpably clear that the mullahs only understand the language of firmness and power. Those who reject a nuclear-armed theocracy and stand with the Iranian people must refrain from appeasing and offering concessions to a murderous religious dictatorship, which is, at the same time the central banker of terrorism and the world record holder in per capita execution of its citizens.

The world community must recognize the rights of the Iranian people to fight for freedom. Accordingly, on behalf of the Iranian people's Resistance, I emphasize:

1 The regime's nuclear program runs counter to the national interests of the Iranian people, who strongly opposed it. In contrast to the mullahs' regime, we seek a democratic, non-nuclear Iran. Out of 80 million Iranians no fewer than 50 million live below the poverty line;

2 Acquiring a nuclear arsenal, abusing human rights, and exporting fundamentalism and terrorism are indispensable features of the ruling theocracy.
Upholding human rights in Iran and forcing the regime to withdraw from Iraq, Syria, Lebanon, Yemen, and Afghanistan offer a real yardstick to ascertain whether or not the regime has abandoned its nuclear weapons program. Anything short, however camouflaged or presented, amounts to self-delusion and acquiesces to the catastrophe of a nuclear-armed theocracy;

NCRI President Remarks in the Congressional Hearing on Islamic Fundamentalism
National Council of Resistance of Iran • U.S. Representative Office (NCRI-US)

3   **Adding six or nine months to the nuclear breakout time while dealing with a regime that has been engaged in a three-decade game of hide and cheat does not provide a solution.** The only guarantee to secure the world from the threat of a nuclear disaster is to fully implement six Security Council resolutions on Iran's nuclear program, completely halt enrichment, and compel the regime to shut down its nuclear sites as well as WMD and missile programs;

4   **Snap inspections anytime, anywhere, of all suspect sites,** military or otherwise, are critical in preventing the mullahs from obtaining the bomb;

5   **The Iranian regime must be obliged to provide satisfactory answers on the possible military dimensions (PMD) of its nuclear projects** (before a final agreement is reached), make available its nuclear experts and documents, and unveil networks involved in smuggling nuclear equipment and material into Iran;

6   **The notion of snapping back the sanctions in the event Tehran violates its commitments or cheats is neither practical nor feasible.** None of the sanctions should be lifted before an agreement has been signed that effectively and definitively denies the mullahs the bomb. Otherwise, the regime will spend billions of unfrozen assets to buy weapons including advanced missiles from Russia.

THE SPREAD OF ISLAMIC FUNDAMENTALISM WAS NOT INEVITABLE

The perceived power of Islamic fundamentalism in general and its epicenter in Tehran in particular, lies neither in its capacity nor its potential to achieve dominance; but is the consequence of the absence of a timely response to this phenomenon. Lack of such a timely response is the by-product of the fact that Islamic fundamentalism has not been properly grasped or understood, something that has led to the adoption of misguided policies. Specifically:

1   Ignoring the threat of Islamic fundamentalism following the collapse of the Soviet Union and the Persian Gulf war in1991.

2   Overlooking that post-9/11 developments in the region overshadowed the role of the epicenter of fundamentalism, i.e., the Iranian regime, giving it the opportunity to implement its plans for spreading extremism in the region.

3   Failing to thwart Tehran's increasing meddling in Iraq after 2003, which led to the gradual hand-over of Iraq to the mullahs. The regime thus received on a silver platter the very prize it could not win during eight years of war with Iraq in the 1980s, despite one million dead, two million wounded and disabled on the Iranian side alone, one trillion dollars in economic damage, and destruction of 3,000 cities and villages.

The mullahs' domination of Iraq, especially under al-Maliki, was the outcome of one of the greatest geopolitical blunders after World War II. It had dire implications for the whole region, including the rise of ISIS and the crises in Syria and Yemen.

4   Disarming and interning the PMOI/MEK (the main Iranian opposition and the only organized, anti-fundamentalist Muslim movement), its subsequent handover to Maliki's puppet regime as well as silence and inaction vis-à-vis repeated attacks on its members in Iraq.

PAGE 22

NCRI President Remarks in the Congressional Hearing on Islamic Fundamentalism
National Council of Resistance of Iran • U.S. Representative Office (NCRI-US)

In addition, the PMOI/MEK and the National Council of Resistance of Iran, (a coalition of democratic forces seeking regime change in Iran) were blacklisted for 15 years, effectively restraining their enormous wherewithal and wasting their resources, which could have otherwise been utilized to effectuate change in Iran. These actions were the best signals to Tehran to continue its efforts to acquire the bomb and export terrorism and fundamentalism with impunity and without having to worry about its popular and legitimate opposition.

A firm policy by the West and support for the Iranian people's aspirations for change and a different approach to the Resistance movement that is the antithesis to the mullahs' fundamentalism would have prevented the spread of extremism and terrorism masquerading as Islam.

The formation of a regional coalition and the launching of Operation Decisive Storm to end the occupation of Yemen by the Iranian regime's proxies was the first such initiative in the past 25 years that acted as an obstacle to the regime's escalating regional meddling.

Time has come to learn from past experience. Since 1993, the Iranian Resistance has been warning about the threat of fundamentalism emanating from the Iranian regime. And since 2003, we have consistently revealed the regime's interference in Iraq. Unfortunately, those warnings have not been heeded.

Today, I reiterate that the mullahs are not part of the solution; they are indeed the heart of the problem.

We must stand up to Tehran's meddling in Iraq. Under no circumstances should the Iraqi militias affiliated with the Iranian regime be legitimized. The solution is to evict the Iranian regime from Iraq.

BARGAINING FOR THE MAXIMUM
TO PRESERVE THE MINIMUM

The mullahs need to export fundamentalism, war, and terror under the banner of Islam beyond Iranian borders to preserve their power in Tehran. One of the essential attributes of fundamentalism is that it can only survive by being on the offensive. Confining the Iranian regime within its own borders and compelling it to abandon its nuclear projects lay bare its real and underlying weaknesses and expedites its downfall.

Khamenei and other regime officials have repeatedly attested to this reality: one step backward is tantamount to retreating all the way back to the overthrow of the state. In December 2014, the Secretary of the regime's Supreme National Security Council, Ali Shamkhani, touched on this point after the killing of one of the most senior commanders of the Quds Force in Iraq. Speaking at his funeral, Shamkhani said, "Those who are sick rumormongers ask us why we interfere in Iraq or Syria. The answer to this question is clear. If [our commanders] do not sacrifice their blood in Iraq, then our blood will be shed in Tehran, Azerbaijan, Shiraz, and Isfahan." Shamkhani emphasized: "To avoid having our blood spilled in Tehran, we must sacrifice our blood in Iraq and defend it."[16]

The 2009 uprising demonstrated that the people of Iran, especially youths and women, are looking for the opportunity to bring fundamental change to Iran. While the Sunni extremists recruit young people in Arab countries and even in some European capitals, in Iran, young people are engaged in a fierce battle against the ruling theocracy. For the past 36 years, the people of Iran have experienced this ominous phenomenon in all its political, social, and economic spheres. An ocean of blood lies between them and the ruling regime.

PAGE 24

NCRI President Remarks in the Congressional Hearing on Islamic Fundamentalism
National Council of Resistance of Iran • U.S. Representative Office (NCRI-US)

The reason is that an organized and cohesive force that adheres to Islam, the PMOI/MEK, promoted in Iranian society a culture of tolerance and belief in freedom. It challenged, with all its might, the violent extremist interpretations of Islam and offered an anti-fundamentalist cultural alternative to Iranian society. Therefore, as the regime becomes weaker and more isolated inside the country it senses a greater need for aggression beyond its borders. Mindful that Islamic fundamentalism has failed in Iran and is detested by the Iranian people, the mullahs have stepped up domestic repression and resorted to terrorism and warmongering as never before in order to preserve their theocracy, misogyny, religious discrimination, or, in a nutshell, maintain their fragile grip on power.

Recall that in the final year of the Second World War, even as the Nazis continued to pose the greatest threat to humanity, they was incapable of preventing the inevitable cracks forming within their rotting core, which rapidly brought its downfall.

THE NEED FOR A CULTURAL AND RELIGIOUS RESPONSE TO FUNDAMENTALISM

An accurate assessment of developments in recent years leads to a very important conclusion that Islamic fundamentalism and extremism are vulnerable and can therefore be defeated. To do so, there is need for a firm comprehensive policy and also a focus on the epicenter, i.e., the regime in Tehran. But reinforcing and increasing intelligence gathering capabilities and intensifying military operations would in and of themselves be insufficient.

A political, religious, and cultural antidote is required to uproot this cancerous tumor permanently. In absence of an alternative interpretation of Islam – which would in fact represent the true spirit of Islam, one that would espouse tolerance, liberty, and freedom of choice for the people, extremist ringleaders will portray the war against fundamentalism as a fight against Islam itself. By doing so, they will then create the most important source of nourishment for this ominous phenomenon. We must demarcate between the true Islam and this rigid reactionary mindset, while exposing and drying up the resources for demagoguery and exploitation of Islam by fundamentalists, especially the Iranian regime. This will not be an easy task and will not come to fruition merely through charming rhetoric.

Fortunately for Iran, the PMOI/MEK is largest political opposition organization and offers a cultural and ideological alternative to Islamic fundamentalism.

Throughout its fifty-year-long history, the PMOI/MEK has posed a political and cultural challenge to Islamic dogmatism. It believes that fundamentalists are ironically the greatest enemies of Islam itself, that their views and conduct have nothing to do with genuine Islam and the Quran and that Islam must be reclaimed.

This organization began to engage in an extensive cultural, social, and political campaign after the fall of the Shah. It was active among the youth in high schools and universities, among women and workers, as well as a wide array of other social sectors and worked to expose the medieval, backward, and anti-democratic nature of Khomeini and his band of clerics. It also introduced democratic Islam. In the course of just 2.5 years, it succeeded in educating a large segment of Iranian society, recruiting them away from the ruling mullahs, before the regime eliminated all peaceful avenues of political activity.

During the first Iranian presidential elections, Massoud Rajavi was the PMOI's candidate, and received widespread support from all social sectors thanks to his adherence to a platform that focused on political and social freedoms that was diametrically opposed to the culture of the Islamic fundamentalism.

Khomeini was so gravely concerned that a majority would cast their ballots to elect Rajavi that he vetoed his candidacy. **According to official counts, Mr. Rajavi received over half a million votes in Tehran during the first parliamentary elections, despite massive electoral fraud.**[17]

PAGE 26

NCRI President Remarks in the Congressional Hearing on Islamic Fundamentalism
National Council of Resistance of Iran • U.S. Representative Office (NCRI-US)

DEMOCRATIC ISLAM:
RESPONSE TO ISLAMIC FUNDAMENTALISM

The Islam to which we adhere is a democratic Islam.

In contrast, the declared objective of Islamic fundamentalism is enforcing Sharia law by force. This goal is the common denominator between the *velayat-e faqih* regime in Iran and Islamic Caliphate of ISIS.

As a Muslim, I declare:

Anything enforced by force and compulsion is not Islam. Neither religion, nor prayer, nor hijab can be enforced through force. As the Holy Quran says, "There is no compulsion in religion."[18]

Freedom is the underlying message of Islam. As the Quran says, Islam has come to free the people from the shackles, not to impose Sharia law.[19]

What fundamentalists present as Sharia law has nothing to do with Islam; it is contrary to the teachings of Islam. The fundamentalists' Sharia law is either self-invented or belongs to the past millennia and only serves them to gain or preserve power. Anything that enchains human beings and deprives them of freedom, choice, and dignity contradicts Islam.

Islam is the religion of compassion and freedom. God Almighty designated the Prophet to be mercy to the worlds.[20]

Islam considers sovereignty to be the greatest right bestowed upon the people. It condemns dictatorship in any form or under any banner. Islam is based on consultation, freedom of choice, expression, and belief.[21]

According to the Quran, people of all races, creeds and genders are equal. Islam defends and encourages human progress and achievements. Consistent with this teaching, the PMOI/MEK has over the past 36 years been advocating democracy, pluralism, and separation of religion and state.

Islam profoundly respects human rights and views the killing of even one man as killing of all of humanity.[22] Islam respects all religions. The Quran insists that there are no differences between prophets.[23]

NCRI President Remarks in the Congressional Hearing on Islamic Fundamentalism
National Council of Resistance of Iran • U.S. Representative Office (NCRI-US)

PAGE 27

This message can defeat Islamic fundamentalism in its most important ideological epicenter. For this reason, democratic and tolerant Islam, which is the true Islam not distorted by the mullahs, is the antithesis to fundamentalism.

By adhering to this mindset, the PMOI/MEK plays a decisive role in the cultural and intellectual defeat of the clerical regime and its isolation within Iran as the godfather of Islamic fundamentalism.

This movement, owing both to its enduring campaign against the religious fascism ruling Iran and paying the enormous cost of this struggle, is uniquely qualified to confront Islamic fundamentalism.

STRATEGY TO OVERCOME FUNDAMENTALISM

With the coming to power of the mullahs in Iran, Islamic extremism emerged as a threat to peace and security. It spread extensively after 2003 when the Iranian regime began to dominate Iraq. So long as the mullahs remain in power in Iran, the crisis will continue in one way or the other.

Thus, the ultimate solution is to overthrow the Iranian regime, which can only be achieved by the people of Iran and Iranian Resistance. However, in order to prevent further deepening of the crisis and putting an end to this catastrophe, the international community needs to take the following steps.

PAGE 28

NCRI President Remarks in the Congressional Hearing on Islamic Fundamentalism
National Council of Resistance of Iran • U.S. Representative Office (NCRI-US)

Take practical measures to evict the Iranian
regime from Iraq.

Only then will fundamentalism begin to retreat, because this is precisely
where it has expanded. The Quds Force, the Shiite militias, and other
proxies of the Iranian regime who have penetrated deep into the political,
military, security, and economic fabric of Iraq during the eight years of
Maliki, must be removed from power structures. It would be a big mistake
to seek the help of these Shiite militias in confronting ISIS. The only
appropriate response to ISIS is to trust, empower, and arm the Sunnis and
engage them in power sharing in a realistic and meaningful way.

2 Help the people of Syria overthrow Bashar Assad and move toward democracy.

The crimes of the Assad regime, which remains in power with the backing
of Tehran and the IRGC, is the greatest cause of Sunni extremists' success
in recruiting volunteers. Had there been a proper response to the Assad
regime's shocking chemical attack in a Damascus suburb, ISIS would have
certainly not been so powerful today. The crimes of the Iranian regime
and Bashar Assad in Syria, which have left hundreds of thousands dead and
more than 10 million people homeless, are the greatest cause of rage and
hatred among Sunni Muslims.

3 Instead of appeasing the heart of fundamentalism and terrorism, i.e., the mullahs' regime, the Iranian people's desire and will to overthrow the clerical regime must be recognized.

Silence vis-à-vis blatant and systematic abuse of human rights and escalating
trend of mass executions in Iran provide the greatest encouragement to
extremists.

A very important part of this approach would be to uphold the rights and guarantee the protection of Camp Liberty residents. Far beyond a humanitarian issue and violation of repeated written commitments by the U.S. and the U.N., the predicament of PMOI/MEK members in Iraq since 2003 has only benefited the Iranian regime and paved the way for expansion of extremism.

As 5.2 million Iraqis declared in a statement in 2006, the PMOI/MEK is the most significant political and cultural bulwark against the spread and penetration of fundamentalism. After the U.S. handed over the protection of Camp Ashraf residents to Iran's puppet regime in Iraq, 116 of residents were killed in six lethal attacks by Iraqi Security Forces. Twenty-five more lost their lives due to an inhumane medical blockade and lack of timely access to medical care. Seven were also taken hostage in 2013, whose fate and whereabouts remain unknown.

4 There must be an emphasis on a democratic and tolerant interpretation of Islam to challenge fundamentalist interpretations whether Shiite or Sunni variants.

5 A decisive policy vis-à-vis the Iranian regime's nuclear program is vital to block its pathways to the bomb.

This would play an important role in eliminating fundamentalism in the region because it would weaken its epicenter and limit the scope of its aggression.

Mr. Chairman,
Distinguished representatives,

Today, the clerical regime is engulfed in deep crisis at home. The people of Iran reject this totalitarian theocracy. They long for freedom, democracy, and regime change.

The Iranian regime is also facing a crippling economic crisis. Corruption has permeated the entire structure of the regime. Official figures say 12 million people go hungry in Iran.[24] Iran has one of the highest inflation rates and the unemployment rate stands at no less than 40 percent.[25] Nevertheless, Rouhani increased the IRGC budget by 50 percent.[26]

Despite a state of absolute repression, protests are spreading by the day. On April 15, one million Iranian teachers staged a nationwide protest in 27 out of 31 provinces. Workers' protests and strikes are also escalating every day.[27]

The proponents of "moderation" within the Iranian regime, such as Rouhani, share the views of other factions regarding the regime's redlines and totalitarian rule of the Supreme Leader. They are partners in domestic repression and exporting terrorism. Contrary to claims by the regime's appeasers, not only are they not a force for change but serve to prolong the velayat-e faqih regime. Comparing them with the opposition to other autocratic regimes is misguided. As long as this regime remains in power, Islamic fundamentalism will persist as the main global threat.

The National Council of Resistance of Iran (NCRI) is a coalition comprised of 500 members, half of whom are women. It consists of democratic forces who seek to overthrow the regime in its entirety and establish a pluralist and secular republic. The NCRI has been waging a resistance against the Iranian regime for 34 years. In addition to a broad-base of support at home, it has gained extensive international recognition and is supported by a wide spectrum of political tendencies in Europe, the United States and Arab and Muslim countries.

According to the NCRI's constitution, a provisional government will be formed for an interim period of only six months after the overthrow of the clerical regime to facilitate the transfer of sovereignty to the people of Iran. It is tasked with holding a free and fair election with international observers, to elect a National Legislative and Constituent Assembly, which will draft a new constitution and run the country's affairs until the constitution of the new republic is ratified.

Consistent with its constitution and ratifications, the NCRI is committed to the Universal Declaration of Human Rights, the International Covenant on Civil and Political Rights, and other relevant international conventions. It is also committed to separation of religion and state and gender equality.

I HAVE OUTLINED THE IRANIAN RESISTANCE'S PLATFORM FOR FUTURE OF IRAN IN THE FOLLOWING 10-POINT PLATFORM:[28]

1 **In our view, the ballot box is the only criterion for legitimacy.** Accordingly, we seek a republic based on universal suffrage.

2 **We want a pluralist system, freedom of parties and assembly.** We respect all individual freedoms. We underscore complete freedom of expression and of the media and unconditional access by all to the Internet.

3 **We are committed to the abolition of death penalty.**

4 **We are committed to separation of Religion and State.** Any form of discrimination against the followers of any religion and denomination will be prohibited.

5 **We believe in complete gender equality in political, social, and economic arenas.** We are also committed to equal participation of women in political leadership. Any form of discrimination against women will be abolished. Women will enjoy the right to select their own clothing and will be free to make their own choices regarding marriage, divorce, education, and employment.

NCRI President Remarks in the Congressional Hearing on Islamic Fundamentalism
National Council of Resistance of Iran • U.S. Representative Office (NCRI-US)

6   **We believe in the rule of law and justice.** We want to set up a modern judicial system based on the principles of presumption of innocence, the right to defense, effective judicial protection, and the right to be tried in a public court. We also seek the total independence of judges. Sharia law will be abolished.

7   **We are committed to the Universal Declaration of Human Rights and international covenants and conventions, including the International Covenant on Civil and Political Rights, the Convention against Torture, and the Convention on the Elimination of all Forms of Discrimination against Women.** We are committed to the equality of all ethnicities. We underscore the plan for the autonomy of Iranian Kurdistan and hold that the language and culture of our compatriots, from whatever ethnicity, are among our nation's precious human resources and must be protected and celebrated in tomorrow's Iran.

8   **We recognize private property, private investment, and the market economy.** All Iranian people must enjoy equal opportunity in employment and in business ventures. We will protect and revitalize the environment.

9   **Our foreign policy will be based on peaceful coexistence,** international and regional peace and cooperation, as well as respect for the United Nations Charter.

10   **We want a non-nuclear Iran, free of weapons of mass destruction.**

Let me conclude my remarks by quoting one of the pioneers of the American civil rights movement, the Reverend Martin Luther King, Jr.: "The arc of the moral universe is long, but it bends towards justice." Our movement has existed before the Iranian Revolution and we have faith that with your help we can move the arc of the moral universe more quickly because our cause is just.

Thank you all very much.

HEARING OF U.S. HOUSE FOREIGN AFFAIRS COMMITTEE

SUBCOMMITTEE ON TERRORISM, NONPROLIFERATION AND TRADE

QUESTIONS & ANSWERS

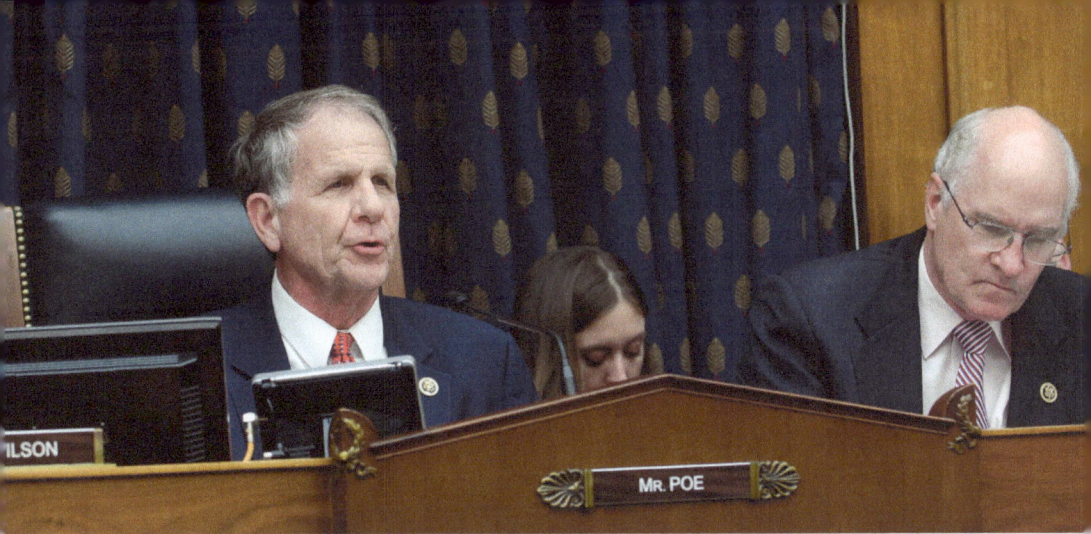

CHAIRMAN TED POE (R-TX)

Thank you Madam Rajavi. We will have questions for you momentarily… I recognize myself for questions. How is ISIS philosophy different from Sunnis, say in Saudi Arabia or Shiites in Iran?

Mrs. RAJAVI: So far as the formation of the ISIS is concerned, it was also the mullahs' regime, which helped the creation of ISIS. The crimes committed by the Iranian regime and Assad and the killing of the Sunnis in Iraq helped the emergence of ISIS.

Therefore, gaining state power, and it was the Iranian regime when there was a state in Iran, created the terrorism as a major threat for security. But from a philosophical respect, the most fundamental element in all fundamentalist groups, whether Sunni or Shi'a, they are common on the following:

They want to force their religion or school of thought, establish a religious dictatorship whether under the name of caliphate or the absolute rule of the clergy, they do not believe in any borders, and go after expansion and capturing other territories and also believe that those who do not accept the Sharia Law must be eliminated.

And I want to stress that there is an antithesis to this philosophy and that is a tolerant and democratic interpretation of Islam. There is a conflict between ISIS and the mullahs in Iran but that is an internal power struggle.

But despite any differences, the continuation of other fundamentalist groups very much hinges on the Iranian regime being in power, remaining in power.

Terrorism and fundamentalism under the name of Islam came to the world scene by the mullahs' regime in Iran and when this regime is overthrown that will be limited or destroyed.

And it is interesting that after the emergence of ISIS, the people of Iran called the Iranian regime the godfather of ISIS.

Regarding Saudi Arabia, I want to add that ISIS, contrary to Saudi Arabia, they do not believe in borders. Therefore, the question is not being Sunni or Salafi or whatever. The problem is those characteristics, which I just identified and that is where you will see that despite all the differences, ISIS is very close to the fundamentalists ruling in Iran. Thank you.

Mr. POE: Mrs. Rajavi, may I ask you a question that you made a comment about? How do you see the mullahs in Iran having facilitated and helped the ISIS movement? How has ISIS been able to expand its influence, its philosophy because of the mullahs in Iran? Make that clear, if you would, on how there is that connection?

Mrs. RAJAVI: As I said, there is a power struggle between ISIS and the regime. But at the same time, on occasions they have cooperated.

For example, Zarqawi, the original founder and leader of ISIS, received enormous logistic support from the Iranian regime and had his bases even in Iran. And I think it was in 2005 that intelligence security services in Germany exposed this connection between Zarqawi and the Iranian regime.

And also there have been many reports even in the media that Bashar al-Assad released many of the ISIS members from prison in order to join ISIS. While in their air attacks they have never attacked ISIS, but the focus is on the moderate opposition in Syria.

So I want to conclude that so far as the mullah's regime in Iran is concerned, they are 100 percent supporting Bashar al-Assad in Syria and therefore all the crimes that are committed by the help and support of the mullah regime has created a fertile ground for ISIS to emerge.

And on the other hand, crimes committed by Maliki at the behest of the Iranian regime in Iraq and in particular the absolute suppression of the Sunnis has led to empowering ISIS to expand itself both in Iraq and Syria.

REP. BRAD SHERMAN (D-CA)

I want to thank the MEK for revealing to the world the Natanz nuclear plant. There may have been a few members of the intelligence committee who knew that before the MEK told us. I was speaking on behalf of roughly 400 members of the Congress. Thank you for telling members of the Congress, as well. Now, you personally promote a very tolerant, moderate view of Islam. You are an advocate of separation of religion and state, and you have been an advocate for human rights and women's rights; of course, your country has been ruled by very rigid laws. They call for stoning people and chopping off limbs. ISIS does the same thing, supposedly in support of a different version of Islam; Iran being Shiite, ISIS being Sunni. Why is their understanding of Islam the same or at least similar in our eyes? And why do both rulers of Iran and ISIS enforce their beliefs through these gruesome measures, if you could respond?

Mrs. RAJAVI: Thank you very much, Congressman Sherman. You touched upon a very important issue. You said that Islamic fundamentalism of the kind of the Shi'ite is even more dangerous than the Sunni one before anything else. The reason is that there is a state empowered in the dimension of the mullahs' regime in a country—in a vast country with so much resources—financial resources and it is supporting these Shi'ite fundamentalist groups financially, ideologically and logistically in every field.

Therefore, they are much more dangerous, I agree with you. Regarding your question as to why they resort to so much violence to pursue their objectives, I should tell you that the reason is they can only survive through absolute terror and fear and this has been the trend of over 30 years of ruling fundamentalists in

Iran that now has expanded to Iraq, Syria, Yemen, Lebanon and other countries. And other fundamentalists take lessons from the Godfather.

Let us not forget that the mullahs in Iran are implementing more than 70 kinds of different tortures—cutting off limbs or gouging out eyes, executing pregnant women and all the heinous crimes that one might imagine and now ISIS and other fundamentalists are really imitating from the mullahs in Iran.
Therefore, I reiterate once again that the ultimate solution is evict, dislodge the Iranian regime from Syria and Iraq and Yemen; and even more important, regime change in Iran.

The fundamentalist regime in Iran must be changed because this regime has created a political umbrella and a source of ideological, logistical and financial support for the fundamentalists and terrorists in today's world.

If it were not due to the destructive influence of the Iranian regime, we would not face the situation today in Iraq, Yemen and Syria, and they would have stability.

Let us not forget that by regime change in Iran, those militia under the command of the Quds Force, like the Hezbollah in Lebanon or Ansar Allah of the Houthis in Yemen and other various groups in Iraq would be eliminated without having their support and they would not have the vital environment, to survive.

Mr. POE: Does the gentleman yield back his time?

Mr. SHERMAN: I would love to ask another question but I have gone over. I yield back.

REP. DANNY DAVIS (D-IL)

Mrs. Rajavi, over the past 30 years the United States has been drawn into some serious diplomatic and military dead ends in the Mideast by mistakenly backing individuals and organizations claiming popular support, which turned out to be largely exaggerated and somewhat manufactured.

Would you please tell us about the role of the National Council of Resistance in Iranian civil life and its place in current Iranian political life, and how do you measure your popular support in Iran?

PAGE 40

NCRI President Remarks in the Congressional Hearing on Islamic Fundamentalism
National Council of Resistance of Iran • U.S. Representative Office (NCRI-US)

Mrs. RAJAVI: With absolute repression, it is not possible to go to the vote of people and see what the people really think, and the mullahs will never accept a free election.

Therefore, the yardstick or the gauge for the popularity of this movement, one, is its persistent continuation of its principles despite the absolute repression and having lost 120,000 of its members and sympathizers who were executed by the regime.

I show you now this book, which includes the names of some 20,000 members of the resistance movement from different strata of the Iranian society. So you can imagine that collecting such information during repression is very difficult.

But another indication is the fear of the regime and its engagement in demonizing the Iranian resistance as another indication of the strength of the resistance and its popularity.

As you may know, in all the diplomatic correspondence that Iran has, its main demand from its interlocutors is to restrict the activities of our movement, and any affiliation with our movement in Iran is equal to execution.

In the 2009 uprising, the regime's officials acknowledged publicly that those demonstrations were organized by the Mujahideen network, the MEK network in Iran and this popular support has enabled this movement also to have access to most secret information of the Iranian regime--on nuclear, on missile and what the Quds Force is doing in the region as well as the human rights violations in Iran.

We have always said to the mullahs' regime that if you really claim that our movement has no popular support, let us have a free election under the auspices of the international community and let us see who has the popular support of the Iranian people. But let us not forget that a free election for the mullahs is a red line.

Mr. DAVIS: Thank you very much.

Mr. POE: With unanimous consent the chair will allow another individual who is not a member of this committee to ask questions. Mrs. Chu from California is recognized.

REP. JUDY CHU (D-CA)

Thank you, Mr. Chair. I would like to address these questions to Mrs. Rajavi. I would like to ask about Camp Liberty. Camp Liberty is a military base that has become a permanent home for over 3,000 Iranian refugees. But the conditions there are poor and freedom is very severely restricted. Worse, there are reports that the Iraqi government is blockading the base, preventing food, water and medicine from arriving.

Combined with the restriction on travel, this blockade has led to at least 25 deaths, the most recent being Mr. Jalal Abedini on April 17th.

Can you give us a sense of living conditions in Camp Liberty in regard to food, medicine and decent housing?

Mrs. RAJAVI: Our prime concern about the residents in Camp Liberty is their safety and security. That is the main problem that they are facing in Camp Liberty now to the extent that since the protection of the residents was transferred from the United States to Iraq, 116 have been killed, seven have been taken hostage and the residents are denied timely access to medical care.

And for this reason, as you have just mentioned, 25 people have lost their lives while there was the possibility to save their life.

I think it was 116 who have been killed during these attacks by Iraqi forces; they have no freedom of movement and enormous restrictions have been imposed on them.

PAGE 42

NCRI President Remarks in the Congressional Hearing on Islamic Fundamentalism
National Council of Resistance of Iran • U.S. Representative Office (NCRI-US)

Just to give you one example, Camp Liberty's electricity is not connected to the city grid and since the Abadi government took office, there have been no changes in the condition and there is still a prison-like situation for the residents.

And I think the new government must recognize Camp Liberty as a refugee camp and remove all the inhumane restrictions, which have been imposed on the camp, and put an end to the daily harassment of the residents.

In particular, it is very important that the camp management be changed because the people who are the camp management are the same people who were engaged in the massacre and the killing of the residents in the past attacks.

And as you know, the United States government had made a written commitment to provide safety and security for these people but that obligation has been violated and I think Camp Liberty should be really put under the protection of the United States or at least their personal weapons to be given so that if they are attacked by the militias or paramilitary groups, they could defend themselves.
And I expect that the United States uphold its commitment to regular monitoring of Camp Liberty.

Mrs. CHU: Let me ask now about—do you have any confidence in the current government to improve conditions, and what is the future for the people at Camp Liberty? Is there a U.S. role?

Mrs. RAJAVI: I think the U.S. government can really demand and urge the Iraqi government to uphold its obligations.

So far, the government has not done anything that we could really trust that they will do the right thing, and as I said the people are still living in a prison-like situation in Camp Liberty as prisoners.

That is why I said that the new government should recognize Liberty as a refugee camp and remove all the restriction imposed on the camp and end the harassment of the residents.

And I want to reiterate that it is very vital to change the camp management and do not allow the mullahs' regime to send its agents for psychological torture of the residents and laying the ground for another massacre in Camp Liberty. These are the actions that they can take and I believe that the United States government is in a position to really call on and demand from the Iraqi government to uphold this obligation. .

Mrs. CHU: Thank you. I yield back.

Mr. POE: I thank the gentlelady. We have also been joined on the dais by the gentlelady from Texas, Mrs. Jackson Lee, and without objection and unanimous consent that she will be allowed to question the witnesses. You have five minutes.

SHEILA JACKSON LEE (D-TX)

Mr. Chairman, thank you very much for your kindness and let me add my appreciation to both you and Ranking Member Sherman and all the members on this panel for their courtesies extended and to indicate that this is a very historic hearing because as far as my memory can recollect, Mr. Chairman, this is one of the few times that the voice of the opposition of the government of Iran has been part of an official discussion.

And that is very important for the American people and for us to formulate the right kinds of policies. Many of us worked for long years to ensure that this great leader, who happens to be a woman, would be able to speak and would be able to lead the MEK and be removed from the terrorist list. There were many machinations and court decisions and we have moved to a decision, which I think reflects the fairness of this nation. Might I also say that the importance of hearing both views in this backdrop of ISIS and the backdrop knows we mean business but, more importantly, this agreement that may come about with Iran is to enhance the security of the United States of America.

To Mrs. Rajavi, I would like to ask the question that you promote a very tolerant and moderate view of Islam. You are an advocate of separation of religion and state and you also favor women's rights and human rights.

Is it true that Iran is holding laws that call for the stoning to death of people and the chopping off of limbs? Can she hear that I was directing that question?

Mr. POE: There is a satellite involved in this communication and it takes a while, plus the translation.

Mrs. JACKSON LEE: Thank you.

Mrs. RAJAVI: Yes, precisely. I should say that what the mullahs really want, they are doing it under the pretext of Islam but it has nothing to do with Islam.

They stone people, amputate limbs and they rape people, and so far, as I said, 120,000 of the best children of the Iranian people have been executed under the name of religion and Islam.

But I should make it clear that Islam is a religion of compassion and freedom and rejects fanaticism, dogmatism and dictatorship. Congresswoman Jackson Lee as you mentioned, we believe in separation of religion and state. We advocate a tolerant and democratic interpretation of Islam, which is the genuine Islam, and we believe that it is the vote of the people that will count.

In our view, there is gender equality between men and women. While, you know that fundamentalists are misogynist, and whatever is based on compulsion is contrary to Islamic teaching.

There is no compulsion in religion, in what you wear, and how you think. And as the Quran said, there is no compulsion in religion. Sovereignty and the vote of people is the treatment… Please, go ahead.

Mrs. JACKSON LEE: Thank you. I am going to make these very brief because I know our time has ended. I just simply know that in the 1979 revolution the Iranian intellectuals called for democracy and human rights.

You just mentioned Islamic fundamentalism, which Iran seems to be the epicenter of, and therefore promoting terrorism. You might want to comment how you think this happened to Iran and then maybe the top challenges that we must face.

If we identify ISIL as an enemy, what are the challenges that relate to freedom, democracy, peace and security that we all want to see? Let me finish by saying that if you have any comments about Camp Liberty and those continued attacks if you want to include that as to how we can work to better stop that, and I would appreciate the chairman's indulgence and I thank you very much for your answers to these questions.

Mrs. RAJAVI: You are absolutely right. The people of Iran wanted freedom and democracy from the revolution and they continue to yearn for freedom and democracy. But, nfortunately, Khomeini stole the leadership of the revolution which was for freedom and democracy and imposed a fundamentalist regime, which by eliminating all freedom and eliminating all political forces from the Iranian society particularly women and the youth, established its rule.

And for the past 37 years, a fundamentalist government has been in power in Tehran. This regime is based on two pillars--export of terrorism and fundamentalism outside and domestic repression, and at the same time trying to acquire nuclear weapons in order to take hostage the international community for doing nothing against these atrocities.
These are the basis or the pillars of this regime. In the month of April, just in this month, nearly 150 executions have been announced in Iran. Only by absolute repression they are maintaining their power.

But on the other hand, there is an organized resistance, which has been resisting this fundamentalist regime for the past 37 years and has been able to expose the fundamentalism and terrorism of this regime and to show the world who is the epicenter of fundamentalism in Iraq, Syria, Lebanon and Yemen and other parts of the world, and to show that where are the secret sites, nuclear secret sites of the mullahs are operating and they have been operating and also to inform the world about the human rights violations In Iran.

But I am absolutely confident that the people of Iran and the Iranian resistance will bring an end, and overthrow this mullahs' regime and bring freedom and democracy for the people of Iran and for the people of the whole region.

And just very briefly about Liberty, as I said, we expect that the United States government upholds its obligations, which has been violated by now and the U.S. government must really put Camp Liberty under its own protection soon and to put an end to the blockade and to demand from the Iraqi government to lift the blockade and to recognize their rights as a "protected person" under the Geneva Conventions. I thank you.

Mrs. JACKSON LEE: Thank you. Thank you very much, Mr. Chairman.

Mr. POE: The gentlelady yields back her time.

Mrs. JACKSON LEE: The gentlelady yields back the time. Thank you.

Mr. POE: I want to thank all of the members of the committee and guests of the committee for being here today. This has been a very insightful hearing and the witnesses have presented three different perspectives…

MEDIA COVERAGE

A SELECTION OF MEDIA REPORTS ON MRS. RAJAVI'S TESTIMONY IN THE U.S. CONGRESS

COVERAGE ARE ALL EXCERPTED FOR THE SAKE OF SPACE

U.S. SENATE SET TO VOTE ON THE IRAN NUCLEAR DEAL OVERSIGHT BILL THIS WEEK

U.S. SENATE SET TO VOTE ON THE IRAN NUCLEAR DEAL OVERSIGHT BILL THIS WEEK

The New York Times

Iranian Opposition Leader:
Tehran Is Force Behind Extremism

April 29, 2015

WASHINGTON, AP — A top Iranian opposition leader told a House subcommittee Wednesday that Iranians have dubbed their government the "godfather" of the Islamic State militant group. Maryam Rajavi, president-elect of the Paris-based National Council of Resistance of Iran, also said Tehran wants nuclear weapons to foster Islamic extremism.

"The ultimate solution to this problem is regime change," Rajavi said.

Testifying before a House Foreign Affairs subcommittee via videoconference from France, Rajavi discussed international negotiations underway to get Iran to curb its nuclear program in exchange for the lifting of economic sanctions crippling its economy. She is the first member of the resistance groups to testify before Congress.

She warned against giving Iran too many concessions, saying it would embolden its leaders to be more aggressive in meddling in other nations.

She said the U.S. and five other nations in talks with Iran must demand that it completely stop enriching uranium and shut down its nuclear sites, missile programs and other programs. While there is no final deal yet, emerging details of an agreement fall short of her demands.

"None of the sanctions should be lifted before an agreement has been signed that effectively and definitively denies the mullahs the bomb," Rajavi said. "Otherwise, the regime will spend billions of unfrozen assets to buy weapons, including advanced missiles from Russia."

NCRI President Remarks in the Congressional Hearing on Islamic Fundamentalism
National Council of Resistance of Iran • U.S. Representative Office (NCRI-US)

THE WALL STREET JOURNAL.

Iranian Dissident Group Back in the Spotlight

April 29, 2015

WASHINGTON— ... In her testimony, Ms. Rajavi said Tehran's regime has been a driving force behind Islamic fundamentalism and extremism from the time it took power in 1979, until the rise of Islamic State, also known as ISIS or ISIL.

"The ultimate solution to this problem is regime change by the Iranian people and Resistance," Ms. Rajavi said. "With the rise of ISIS and escalation of the crises in Iraq, Syria and Yemen, Islamic extremism has grown more vexing in recent months. But, for the Iranian people and Resistance, this was not an unknown peril."

Much of the hearing room attention was focused on Ms. Rajavi's first appearance under oath, and the organizations with which she is linked.

Rep. Brad Sherman (D., Calif.) defended Ms. Rajavi's invitation and likened her appearance to one Wednesday by Japanese Prime Minister Shinzo Abe. Mr. Sherman said that, in the past, Japan had carried out horrific actions against American prisoners of war, but "that was then."

Mr. Sherman dismissed concerns that her testimony could help legitimize the group. "I've been here almost 20 years, heard about 16,000 witnesses," he said. "I've never heard a witness that wasn't providing information to further her public policy interests."...

The Washington Post

Seeking to Understand Islamic State, Congress Hears from Foe of Iran

April 30, 2015

A controversial foe of the Iranian government sought to tie the rise of the Islamic State terrorist group to the regime in Iran before Congress on Wednesday — a link that President Obama and many foreign policy experts have rejected but one that has gained traction on Capitol Hill as Obama continues nuclear talks with Iran.

A House foreign affairs subcommittee's decision to invite Maryam Rajavi, a longtime leader of Mujaheddin-e Khalq, had generated objections before the hearing. The exile group, also known as MEK, was listed as a terrorist organization by the State Department as recently as 2012 and had been known to ally itself with Iraqi dictator Saddam Hussein against Tehran.

But since the group formally renounced violence, the most aggressive U.S. foes of the Iranian regime have embraced MEK as an ally. With Wednesday's hearing on the Islamic State, that alliance has been extended to discussions of the Sunni extremist group now attracting the attention of lawmakers as it wreaks havoc in the Middle East.

 "The mullahs' regime is not part of the solution to the current crisis," Rajavi said, referring to the Iranian government. "It is indeed the heart of the problem." The regime in Tehran is the "godfather" of the Islamic State, she said, adding that "the ultimate solution to this problem is regime change by the Iranian people and resistance."...

Rajavi testified as president-elect of the National Council of Resistance of Iran, MEK's political affiliate. She appeared before the subcommittee on terrorism, nonproliferation and trade via video link from Paris.

NCRI President Remarks in the Congressional Hearing on Islamic Fundamentalism
National Council of Resistance of Iran • U.S. Representative Office (NCRI-US)

AP

Iranian Opposition Leader: Tehran is Force Behind Extremism

April 29, 2015

WASHINGTON — A top Iranian opposition leader told a House subcommittee Wednesday that Iranians have dubbed their government the "godfather" of the Islamic State militant group.

Maryam Rajavi, president-elect of the Paris-based National Council of Resistance of Iran, also said Tehran wants nuclear weapons to foster Islamic extremism.

"The ultimate solution to this problem is regime change," Rajavi said. Testifying before a House Foreign Affairs subcommittee via videoconference from France, Rajavi discussed international negotiations underway to get Iran to curb its nuclear program in exchange for the lifting of economic sanctions crippling its economy. She is the first member of the resistance groups to testify before Congress.

She warned against giving Iran too many concessions, saying it would embolden its leaders to be more aggressive in meddling in other nations.

She said the U.S. and five other nations in talks with Iran must demand that it completely stop enriching uranium and shut down its nuclear sites, missile programs and other programs. While there is no final deal yet, emerging details of an agreement fall short of her demands.

"None of the sanctions should be lifted before an agreement has been signed that effectively and definitively denies the mullahs the bomb," Rajavi said. "Otherwise, the regime will spend billions of unfrozen assets to buy weapons, including advanced missiles from Russia."

U.S.News & WORLD REPORT

MEK Uses Congressional Spotlight to Push Regime Change in Iran

April 30, 2015

The Iranian dissident group's leader told lawmakers that Tehran's mullahs are an inspiration for Islamists everywhere.

WASHINGTON — MEK leader Maryam Rajavi told lawmakers on April 29 that the path to defeating the Islamic State (IS) runs through regime change in Tehran.

Testifying by teleconference from the exiled group's headquarters in Paris, Rajavi urged the United States to stand up to Iran throughout the region. Her appearance has sparked controversy because the MEK was listed as a terrorist group until 2012, but several lawmakers defended her right to testify and held up her organization as a viable democratic alternative to the mullahs.

"Since [1979], the regime in Tehran has acted as the driving force for, and the epicenter of, this ominous phenomenon regionally and worldwide," Rajavi testified before the House Foreign Affairs Committee's panel on Terrorism, Nonproliferation and Trade. "The ultimate solution to this problem is regime change by the Iranian people and resistance."

"This is a very historic hearing," said Jackson Lee, who along with panel Chairman Ted Poe, R-Texas, actively pressed the State Department to take the MEK off its terrorism list. "This is one of the few times that the voice of the opposition [to] the government of Iran has been part of an official discussion. And that's very important for the American people." ...

Freshman Rep. Lee Zeldin, R-N.Y., left little doubt that he believed in her.

PAGE 54

NCRI President Remarks in the Congressional Hearing on Islamic Fundamentalism
National Council of Resistance of Iran • U.S. Representative Office (NCRI-US)

"I honestly do not know if my president is on the same exact team that I am," he told Rajavi. "Because there are individuals like you, who are willing to rise up and take control of your country's future."

Rep. Brad Sherman, D-Calif., said the MEK's terrorism designation belonged in the past and compared Rajavi's appearance to Japanese Prime Minister Shinzo Abe's address to Congress earlier in the day. He said the media had "attacked" the MEK's inclusion in the hearing because she was advocating for a certain policy — namely, regime change — but argued that most if not all other witnesses do the same.

"I've never heard a witness that wasn't providing information to further their public policy interests," Sherman said...

Iran 'Godfather' of IS Jihadists: Opposition Leader

April 29, 2015

Washington (AFP) — The leader of an exiled Iranian opposition group addressed US lawmakers for the first time Wednesday and warned of the links between Shiite Iran and the Sunni Muslim Islamic State (IS) militants.

"It was the mullahs' regime who helped the creation of ISIS... and the killing of Sunnis in Iraq helped the emergence of ISIS," Maryam Rajavi told House lawmakers, using another acronym for the IS jihadist group that has captured a swathe of territory in Iraq and Syria.

Rajavi is the president-elect of the National Council of Resistance of Iran, a political umbrella coalition of five Iranian opposition groups that includes the once blacklisted People's Mujahedin of Iran (MEK).

Although Iran has been helping Iraqi leaders to fight the Sunni IS militants by arming and advising Shiite militias, Rajavi insisted that Iranians called Iran's religious leaders "the godfather" of IS.

"It was the Iranian regime ... that created terrorism as a major threat for stability," Rajavi said, appearing at the House foreign affairs committee via a live satellite link from her Paris offices.

"Terrorism and fundamentalism under the name of Islam came to the world as seen by the mullahs' regime in Iran, and when this regime is overthrown, that will be limited or destroyed."

And she alleged that "despite all their differences, ISIS is very close to the fundamentalists ruling in Iran" and even on "occasions they have cooperated."

"The mullahs' regime is not part of any solution as we attempt to deal with Islamic fundamentalism. It is indeed the heart of the problem," she added, insisting the "ultimate solution" was regime change in Iran.

NCRI President Remarks in the Congressional Hearing on Islamic Fundamentalism
National Council of Resistance of Iran • U.S. Representative Office (NCRI-US)

Iran 'Godfather' of ISIS Militants: Opposition Leader

April 30, 2015

"It was the mullahs' regime who helped the creation of ISIS... and the killing of Sunnis in Iraq helped the emergence of ISIS," Maryam Rajavi told House lawmakers.

"It was the Iranian regime ... that created terrorism as a major threat for stability," Rajavi said, appearing at the House foreign affairs committee via a live satellite link from her Paris offices.

"Terrorism and fundamentalism under the name of Islam came to the world as seen by the mullahs' regime in Iran, and when this regime is overthrown, that will be limited or destroyed."

And she alleged that "despite all their differences, ISIS is very close to the fundamentalists ruling in Iran" and even on "occasions they have cooperated."

"The mullahs' regime is not part of any solution as we attempt to deal with Islamic fundamentalism.

It is indeed the heart of the problem," she added, insisting the "ultimate solution" was regime change in Iran.

THE
HILL

Why America Must Embrace the Iranian Resistance

By former Rep. Patrick J. Kennedy (D-R.I.)

May 1, 2015

This past Wednesday could well mark a turning point in the U.S.'s fight against ISIS and other forces of instability and violence in the greater Middle East. The House Foreign Affairs Subcommittee on Terrorism, Non-Proliferation, and Trade held a hearing entitled "ISIS: Defining the Enemy," where Maryam Rajavi, the president-elect of the Iranian opposition group the National Council of Resistance of Iran (NCRI), was the first to testify.

This is a watershed development, especially at a moment when the U.S. government is flying headlong into a nuclear deal with Tehran that can only help legitimize the brutal Iranian theocracy that is fomenting much of the sectarian chaos that is feeding the rise of ISIS.

In her remarks, provided via videoconference from Paris, Rajavi offered an alternate reality scenario of an Iran that is secular, non-nuclear, and democratic. Such a nation not only would reduce the existential dread of our allies in the region, but would drain the swamp of Iran's terrorist proxies such as Hezbollah which have sparked the vicious Sunni extremist backlash led by Al Qaeda and ISIS. This makes groups like NCRI promising allies in the fight against Islamic extremism. We need to encourage and empower progressive and anti-fundamentalist Muslim groups like NCRI and I urge my former colleagues in Congress to heed what Rajavi said.

The U.S. may already be feeling the first pangs of buyer's remorse from its negotiations with Tehran as our warships arrive in the Persian Gulf in a show of strength against Iran's toppling of a pro-Western government in Yemen. Tehran's terrorist proxies are filling the power vacuum in Sana, a fact that has spawned an entirely predictable counter-reaction from Al Qaeda. Chaos and the danger of a spreading anti-American terrorist threat in Yemen have shaken the region and the U.S. national security establishment.

NCRI President Remarks in the Congressional Hearing on Islamic Fundamentalism
National Council of Resistance of Iran • U.S. Representative Office (NCRI-US)

America and the West face a grave choice. We can continue to acquiesce and accommodate Tehran, loosening sanctions, injecting money into its faltering economy, and legitimizing its leadership with diplomatic victories. Or we can confront the reality of a hegemonic, nuclear-threshold state driven by fundamentalist zeal.

The appearance of NCRI before the Congress today should give us hope that democracy and freedom still have a place in the U.S.' foreign policy priorities for the greater Middle East. Rajavi's organization is the most prominent and effective political group calling for regime change in Iran, and have proven their mettle to U.S. policymakers by helping reveal the details of the Iranian nuclear program. They have been warning of the global threat of Islamic fundamentalism since at least the early 1990s. Rajavi's voice is even more important today because the Obama administration is embracing Tehran even as the U.S. State Department still regards the clerical regime as the world's number one state sponsor of terrorism.

If we are serious about defeating ISIS, we must not empower Iran, an equally potent source of Islamic fundamentalism and the sworn enemy of the United States for 36 years. The U.S. government's desire for short-term, low-investment political solutions has consistently allowed the Iranian regime to degrade the Iranian resistance. NCRI members and other brave Iranian dissidents have been systematically hunted, imprisoned, and executed in an escalating parade of atrocities documented by Human Rights Watch and other NGOs.

That a confident, visionary Iranian woman addressed a key committee of the U.S. Congress should not be lost on the Obama administration or the ayatollahs running the show in Tehran. Iran is still a country where women are routinely stoned to death for a litany of offenses against the theocracy. Rajavi thus spoke as much for the U.S. as she did for the country she hails from. It is time for America to embrace the Iranian opposition as a matter of urgent national interest. It is essential to the defeat of Islamic extremism. And it is consistent with our deepest held values.

Kennedy served in the House from 1995 to 2011. He is the son of late former Sen. Ted Kennedy (D-Mass.).

NCRI President Remarks in the Congressional Hearing on Islamic Fundamentalism

Mrs. Maryam Rajavi

Mrs. Maryam Rajavi is the President-elect of the National Council of Resistance of Iran, which seeks the establishment of a democratic, secular and non-nuclear republic in Iran.

As a Muslim woman, she advocates tolerance, gender equality and separation of religion and state.

Mrs. Rajavi was politically active during and after the 1979 revolution. She received a Bachelor's degree in Metallurgical Engineering in Sharif University of Technology in Tehran.

She was a candidate during the first parliamentary elections after the revolution and received approximately a quarter million votes, despite widespread election fraud by the Iranian regime.

Mrs. Rajavi has appeared before many national parliaments in Europe, including the United Kingdom, Germany, Italy, Spain, Belgium, Switzerland, the Netherlands, Norway, Finland, Canada and has been a frequent guest at the European Parliament and the Parliamentary Assembly of the Council of Europe as well as France's National Assembly and the Senate, where she has testified.

Her latest book, entitled, Woman against Islamic Fundamentalism, has been translated into several languages.

Mrs. Rajavi lost two of her sisters in the struggle to bring freedom and democracy to Iran. One, pregnant at the time, was executed by ayatollahs' regime. Another was executed by the Shah's regime. One of her brother-in-laws was executed in Iran and another was assassinated by the Iranian regime's terrorists in Geneva, Switzerland.

National Council of Resistance of Iran (NCRI)

National Council of Resistance of Iran (NCRI), a broad coalition of democratic Iranian organizations, groups and personalities, was founded in 1981 in Tehran upon the initiative of Massoud Rajavi, the Leader of the Iranian Resistance.

The NCRI has more than 500 members, including representatives of ethnic and religious minorities such as the Kurds, Baluchis, Armenians, Jews and Zoroastrians, representing a broad spectrum of political tendencies in Iran. Acting as parliament in exile, the NCRI aims to establish a democratic, secular and coalition government in Iran. Women comprise 50% of the council's members.

All members of the Council have one vote. All decisions are adopted by a simple majority.

The council's 25 committees form the basis for a provisional coalition government once the mullahs are toppled. Chairing each committee is a prominent political personality who is an expert in the field.

The provisional government will be in power for only six months and its main responsibility is to hold free and fair elections for a National Legislative and Constituent Assembly and to transfer power to the representatives of the people of Iran.

National Solidarity Front, a leap forward

In 2002, NCRI adopted a plan to form the "National Solidarity Front to Overthrow Religious Dictatorship in Iran." The front was designed as a platform to encompass all Iranian who believe in a republican system of government and "are campaigning for a democratic, independent and secular regime."

The Council noted that brightening prospects for overthrow of the regime necessitate ever-greater national solidarity among Iranians; a fact that prompted the NCRI to ratify the formation of the Front.

Mrs. Maryam Rajavi described the Front as "a reflection of the most profound democratic yearnings of all the people of Iran, regardless of ideology, belief, religion and ethnicity that transcends all partisan and political interests." She said the Front "embodies the unshakable resolve of the Iranian people to overthrow the mullahs' inhuman regime."

ENDNOTES

[1] Mohammad Mohaddessin, "Islamic Fundamentalism: The New Global Threat", 1st edition, (Seven Locks Press: 1993). Available at Amazon.com.

[2] The Constitution of the Islamic Republic of Iran, Article 150. The Islamic Revolutionary Guards Corps, organized in the early days of the triumph of the Revolution, is to be maintained so that it may continue in its role of safeguarding the Revolution and its achievements.

[3] *Fallen for Freedom, 20,000 PMOI Martyrs – Partial List of 120,000 Victims of Political Executions in Iran under the Mullahs' Regime.* Compiled by the People's Mojahedin Organization of Iran on the Forty-first Anniversary of its Foundation – September 2006.

[4] The Constitution of the Islamic Republic of Iran, Article 3, no. 16: Framing the foreign policy of the country on the basis of Islamic criteria, fraternal commitment to all Muslims, and unsparing support to the *Mustazafan* [abased] of the world Article 11: ...the government of the Islamic Republic of Iran has the duty of formulating its general policies with a view to cultivating the friendship and unity of all Muslim peoples, and it must constantly strive to bring about the political, economic, and cultural unity of the Islamic world. Article 154: while scrupulously refraining from all forms of interference in the internal affairs of other nations, it supports the just struggles of the *Mustazafan* (the abased) against the *Mustakberan* (oppressors) in every corner of the globe.

[5] Mojahed weekly publication, No. 427, February 9, 1999 – Containing the list of names and particulars of 3,208 massacred political prisoners.

[6] Mostafa Pourmohammadi, representative of the Intelligence Ministry in the Death Commission that was in charge of the massacre of political prisoners in 1988, is now the Minister of Justice in Rouhani's cabinet.

[7] Khamenei's sermon at Tehran's Friday prayer, February 3, 2012: "We believe that Muslims, whether Sahfeii, Jaafari, Maleki, Hanbali or Zaidi, are all Islamic sects who are brothers and must have mutual respect for one another. They should have healthy, fraternal dialogues in Fiq'h, interpretation of words and history and work hand in hand to build a single, powerful, global Islamic Civilization of the Prophet Mohammad (S.A.W) in the contemporary time.

"Iran seeks not to make Arabs Persian or make Shiites out of other Muslims. Iran seeks to advocate the Quran and the tradition of the Prophet Mohammad (SAW) and his household (SAW) and revitalize the Islamic nation. For the Islamic Revolution there is a religious obligation and duty to assist the Sunni jihadists of the Hamas organizations as well as the Shiite jihadists of the Hezbollah on an equal level." (Iranian state-run News Network TV, February 3, 2012)

[8] Khamenei's speech at Khomeini's grave: "Today, some people in different parts of the world of Islam - which go by the name of Takfiri, Wahhabi and Salafi groups - are adopting bad and inappropriate measures against Iran, Shia Muslims and Shia Islam. But everyone should know that they are not the main enemies." (Iran's state-run News Network TV, June 4, 2014)

[9] Khomeini's last will, article F:
You, the meek of the world and Islamic countries and the world's Muslim, rise up and obtain your rights with empty hands. Do not fear the propaganda of the super powers and their subservient lackeys. Expel the criminal rulers who surrender your earnings to your enemies and the enemies of dear Islam

¹⁰ Shob'heh website: Why is His Excellency, the leader, referred to as "the leader of the world's Muslims"?
  a. Not only is there a difference between a source of emulation and a ruler of an Islamic Government, but there is also a difference between a "decree" and a "fatwa". It is an obligation for the followers of a certain source of emulation to abide by his fatwa, whereas if a religious authority issues a "decree," all Shiites and even the authorities are obliged to follow it. (Like the decree issued by Mirza Shirazi boycotting tobacco)
  b. Therefore, under the rule of a religious authority, it is an obligation to abide by his governmental orders. Therefore, he is their Imam and their leader.
  c. Today, there are two billion Muslims in the world. Nearly 500 million of them are Shiites. Therefore, in light of the fact that it is an obligation for all Muslims to follow the orders of "the Guardian of all Muslims" or "the Velayat-e Faqih" (absolute clerical rule), it is clear that he is the leader of all Muslims around the world.

¹¹ Khomeini's speech on the anniversary of the birth of the Prophet of Islam In 1982.

¹² A Majlis (parliament) deputy said on September 18, 2014: Currently, there are three Arab capitals in the hands of Iran and Sana'a [in Yemen] will the fourth capital…We are seeking to integrate all Islamic countries."

¹³ Khamenei's representative and the Friday prayer leader of Zanjan province said: The boundaries of the Islamic Republic are in Yemen and attacking Yemen is the same as attacking the Islamic Republic." IRNA, state-run news agency, April 17, 2015.

¹⁴ Mullah Mehdi Ta'eb, Khamenei's chief advisor: "Syria is the 35th province of the country and a strategic province for us." Fars News Agency, February 14, 2013.

¹⁵ Given the increase in population and growing demand for cars on a per capita basis, Iran is in need of gasoline and is one of the biggest importers of fuel.

NAME OF REFINERY	DAILY PRODUCTION CAPACITY	DAILY PRODUCTION OF GAS (LITER/DAY)
Abadan	9138	1291
Tehran	1700	1348
Kermanshah	1137	1350
Shiraz	1905	352
Lavan	987	1355
Tabriz	2884	1327
Isfahan	7568	1357
Arak	4760	1372
Bandar Abbas	13000	1376

(BBC, August 30, 2011)

¹⁶ Ali Shamkhani, secretary of the Supreme Security Council: "There are sick people who spread rumors these days, asking about the connection between Samara [in Iraq] and Hamid Taqavi. They ask what do we have to do with Iraq and Syria? The answer to this question is clear. If the likes of Taqavi do not give their blood in Samara, then we would have our blood shed in Sistan, Azerbaijan, Shiraz and Isfahan." Fars News Agency, December 29, 2014.

¹⁷ The Election Results, Ettela'at Newspaper, 13 April 1980.

¹⁸ The Holy Quran, Chapter 2, Baqarah (Cow), verse 256.

[19] The Holy Quran, Chapter 7, *Al-A'raf* (The Heights), verse 157.

[20] The Holy Quran, Chapter 21, *Al-Anbya* (The Prophets), verse 107.

[21] The Holy Quran, Chapter 42, *Ash-Shura* (The Consultation), verse 38; Chapter 3, *Ali Imran* (Family of Imran), verse 159.

[22] The Holy Quran, Chapter 5, *Al-Maidah* (The Table Spread), verse 32.

[23] The Holy Quran, Chapter 2, *Baqarah* (Cow), verse 285.

[24] Ali Rabii, Minister of Cooperation, Labor and Social Affairs – Mehr News Agency, December 5, 2014.

[25] Iranian Economy Website – November 18, 2014.

[26] Iranian Fiscal Year Budget 1394 (March 2015 – March 2016) – Eghtesad News, January 7, 2015.

[27] The Associated Press. April 16, 2015: "Iran's semi-official ILNA news agency says thousands of teachers have staged nationwide protests demanding higher wages. The report says peaceful protests were held Thursday in several cities, including the capital, Tehran. It says the teachers gathered in silence in front of provincial Education Ministry buildings. In Tehran, hundreds of teachers gathered in front of parliament. The protesters carried placards in which they asked for higher wages and demanded the release of teachers allegedly detained in similar protests last month."

[28] Maryam Rajavi's vision for the future of Iran – June 22, 2013. Available at Maryam-Rajavi.com/en.

www.ingramcontent.com/pod-product-compliance
Lightning Source LLC
Chambersburg PA
CBHW040930030426
42334CB00002B/22